Especially for
With love from

For Lily, Ginny, and Molly

—Jordan

For Mum

—Jonathan

The Spirit in You

Written by Jordan Raynor • Illustrated by Jonathan D. Voss

BIBLE

Raynor · Voss
The Creator in You

Raynor · Voss
ROYAL in YOU

HAVE YOU EVER DONE SOMETHING
you knew that you shouldn't?

Or something a grown-up said that you couldn't?

Everyone has, whether they're ninety or seven.

These things are called sins by our Father in heaven.

Sin is when we choose to disobey,
when we ignore God's rules and go our own way.

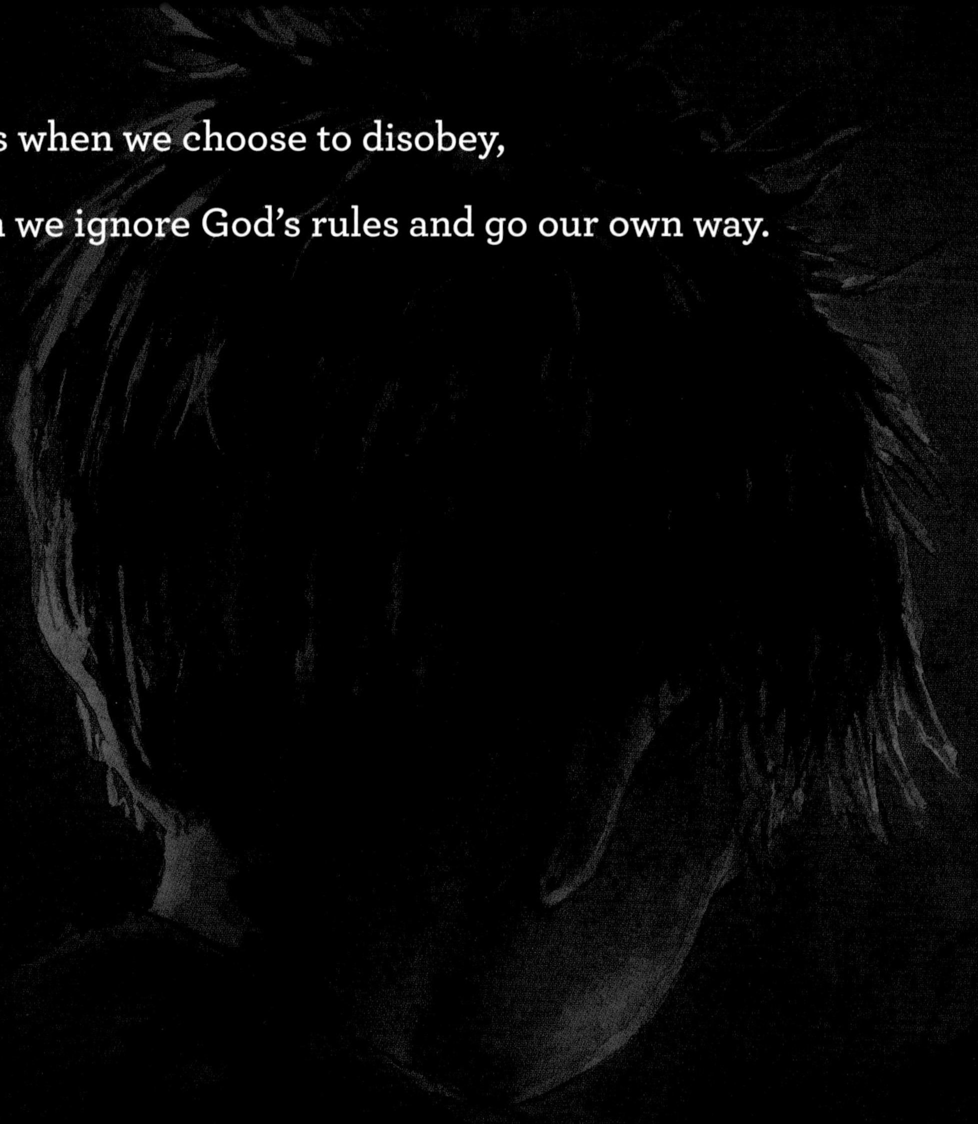

The punishment for sin, if we don't turn around,
is God letting us choose to stay lost and not found.
It's being without Him for all of eternity,
far away from His love and all of His family.

EPH
2:10

That is the bad news. But here is the good!

Jesus took the punishment that you and I should.

He died on a cross for the bad things we've done

and rose from the dead, proving He is God's Son.

And now Jesus offers forgiveness of sins—
the way back to God from wherever you've been.
This way can't be bought like a toy at the store
or earned through good works like being kind to the poor.

BIBLE

You just must confess and admit that you've sinned
and that Jesus alone can make you right again,
then declare with your mouth that Jesus is Lord
who is worthy of being obeyed and adored.

Once you do that, you'll be with God forever.

At your church, on a plane—whenever, wherever.

How is that possible? How can it be true?

God sends His Holy Spirit to live *inside* you.

And now you might think that our story is ending,

but in fact, this is just the beginning.

Because while your good works did nothing to *save* you,

they *are* what God's Spirit gives you power *to* do.

Like caring less for yourself and more about others—

your neighbors and classmates and sisters and brothers.

And making the world a more beautiful place

in ways that bring joy and a smile to God's face.

And taking great care of this earth God calls good
by recycling or planting a tree in the woods.

The Spirit in you works for justice for all—

at school, on the playground, and at city hall.

And helps you discover the world's greatest mysteries,

which lead you to worship the God of all history.

And gives you the power to do homework and chores

as if you were doing those things for the Lord.

He leads you to share the good news with everyone

that Jesus loves us, no matter what bad we've done.

FOR GOD SO
LOVED

Jesus loves you the same without your good deeds,

but I hope that by now you are starting to see

that the Spirit is not just for *your* salvation

but to help you do good for *all* of creation.

And when you show others the Spirit in you,

you'll be doing the good that God saved you to do.

Note to Parents

I wrote *The Spirit in You* because I wanted a book that succinctly and winsomely communicated the path to *and* purpose of salvation for my kids and yours.

You may have noticed that this book is structured into two halves.

The first half focuses on the *path* to salvation and is essentially an exposition of EPHESIANS 2:8–9, where the apostle Paul says, "It is by grace you have been saved, through faith—and this is not from yourselves, it is the gift of God—not by works, so that no one can boast."

Salvation by grace is what makes Christianity so beautiful and dazzlingly different from every other religion. But if we're not careful, our preaching of the gospel can focus exclusively on what God has saved our kids *from* while saying nothing about what God has saved them *for*.

That's why I spend the entire second half of *The Spirit in You* focused on the *purpose* of our salvation, which Paul articulates

beautifully in EPHESIANS 2:10, saying that "we are God's handiwork, created in Christ Jesus *to do good works,* which God prepared in advance for us to do." In other words, "while your good works did nothing to *save* you, they *are* what God's Spirit gives you power *to* do."

Paul is saying that part of the purpose of our salvation is to get back to the "good works, which God prepared in advance" for humankind to do in the Garden of Eden—namely to "fill the earth" with beautiful things "that bring joy and a smile to God's face," to "subdue" the earth by working to "discover the world's greatest mysteries," and to "rule" with Christ by sharing "the good news with everyone" that God longs to be with them.

Friends, the good news of the gospel is not just that our kids get to go to heaven when they die but also that they get to work to bring heaven to earth their entire lives.

I pray this book leaves your kids *amazed* by grace and the path to salvation found in Christ alone. And I pray it leaves them feeling *empowered* by the purpose of their salvation—to "do good for *all* of creation" through the power of the Holy Spirit.

To further cultivate that amazement and empowerment in your kids, check out the free devotional I've written for you and your children to read together at www.jordanraynor.com/kids.